I0813259

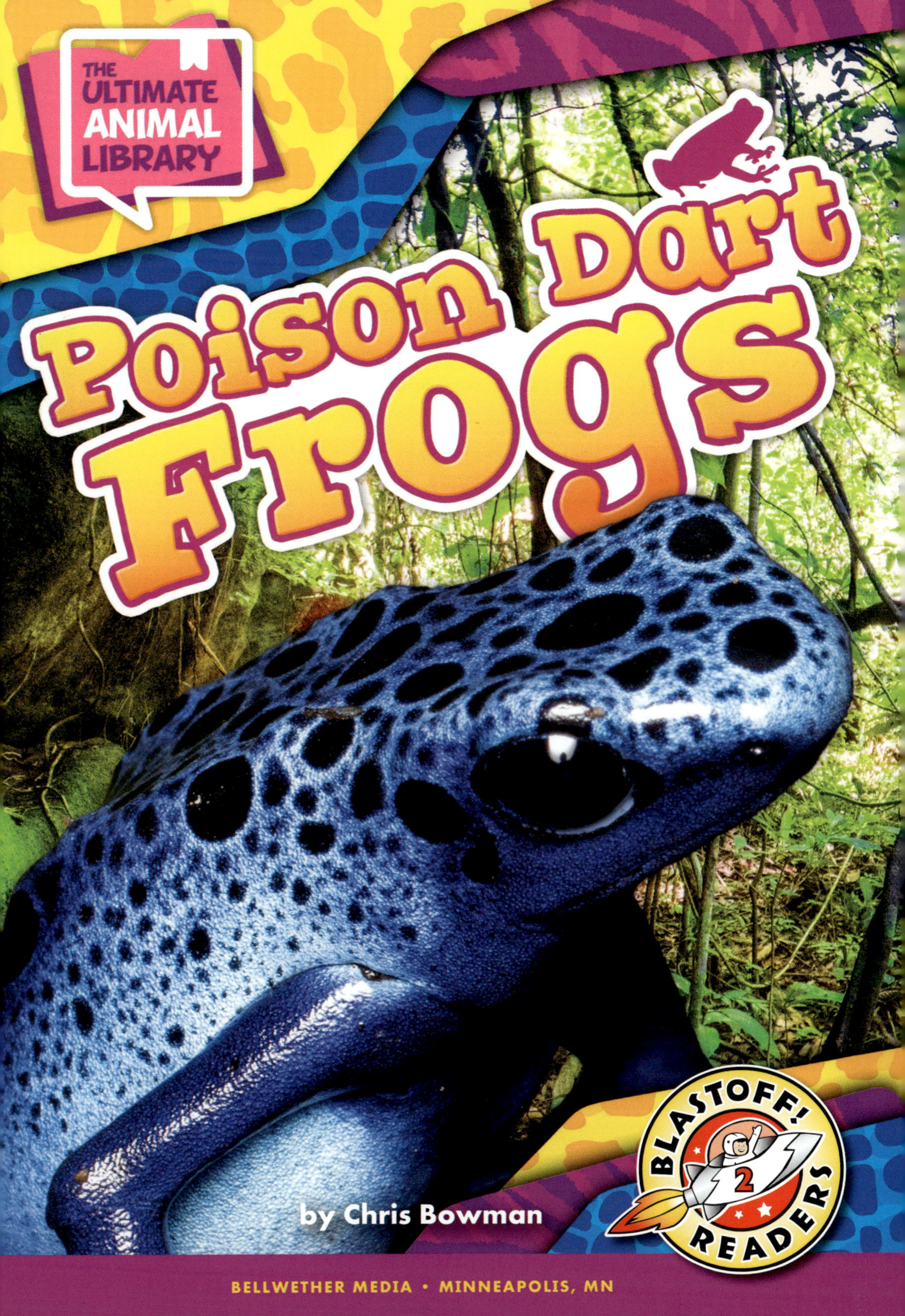
THE ULTIMATE ANIMAL LIBRARY
Poison Dart Frogs
by Chris Bowman
BLASTOFF! READERS
2
BELLWETHER MEDIA • MINNEAPOLIS, MN

Blastoff! Readers are carefully developed by literacy experts to build reading stamina and move students toward fluency by combining standards-based content with developmentally appropriate text.

Level 1 provides the most support through repetition of high-frequency words, light text, predictable sentence patterns, and strong visual support.

Level 2 offers early readers a bit more challenge through varied sentences, increased text load, and text-supportive special features.

Level 3 advances early-fluent readers toward fluency through increased text load, less reliance on photos, advancing concepts, longer sentences, and more complex special features.

★ **Blastoff! Universe**

Reading Level

BLASTOFF! Beginners
Grade K

Grades 1–3

Grade 4

This edition first published in 2026 by Bellwether Media, Inc.

Library of Congress Cataloging-in-Publication Data

LC record for Poison Dart Frogs available at: https://lccn.loc.gov/2025003946

Editor: Elizabeth Neuenfeldt   Series Designer: Veah Demmin

Printed in the United States of America, North Mankato, MN.

Table of Contents

What Are Poison Dart Frogs?

Poison dart frogs are small **amphibians**. They live in Central and South America. They are known for their bright colors. They stand out against trees.

Golden Poison Frog Report

Range

Status in the Wild

endangered

Habitat

rain forests

The colors of poison dart frogs warn **predators** that they are dangerous to eat.

The frogs have poison in their skin. Touching them can be deadly.

These frogs are small.
Most are less than 1 inch
(2.5 centimeters) long.

Some grow up to 2.4 inches (6 centimeters) long.

Poison dart frogs have big eyes. They can see tiny **insects**. Sticky tongues help them catch **prey**.

The bottoms of their toes are sticky. This helps the frogs climb.

Spot a Poison Dart Frog

tongue

Poison dart frogs call **rain forests** home.

They rest on leaves or in logs.
They are often near water.

Poison dart frogs are active during the day. Sunlight makes their colors stand out.

fire-bellied snake

Their colors keep most predators away. But fire-bellied snakes hunt them.

Poison dart frogs eat many kinds of insects.

They often eat ants and beetles. They also eat small flies.

Growing Up

Female poison dart frogs lay eggs. Some **species** lay up to 40 eggs at once.

One parent guards the eggs until they **hatch**. Then the parent moves their **tadpoles** to water.

eggs

tadpoles

The tadpoles grow front legs after about eight weeks. Their colors change two weeks later.

Time to move to land!

Life of a Poison Dart Frog

Name of Babies

tadpoles

Number of Eggs

up to 40

Time Spent in Eggs

around 2 weeks

Life Span

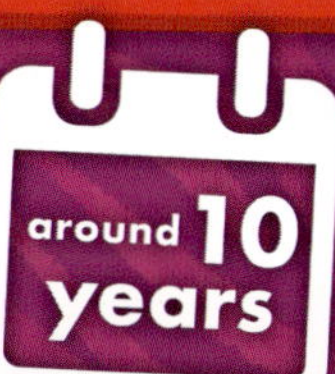

around 10 years

Glossary

amphibians—animals that are able to live both on land and in water

hatch—to break open

insects—small animals with six legs and bodies divided into three parts

predators—animals that hunt other animals for food

prey—animals that are hunted by other animals for food

rain forests—thick, green forests that receive a lot of rain

species—kinds of an animal

tadpoles—baby poison dart frogs

To Learn More

AT THE LIBRARY

Hansen, Grace. *Poison Dart Frogs.* Minneapolis, Minn.: Abdo Kids, 2023.

Neuenfeldt, Elizabeth. *Frog.* Minneapolis, Minn.: Bellwether Media, 2021.

Sabelko, Rebecca. *Rain Forest Animals.* Minneapolis, Minn.: Bellwether Media, 2023.

ON THE WEB

FACTSURFER

Factsurfer.com gives you a safe, fun way to find more information.

1. Go to www.factsurfer.com.
2. Enter "poison dart frogs" into the search box and click 🔍.
3. Select your book cover to see a list of related content.

Index

The images in this book are reproduced through the courtesy of: Jason Mintzer, cover (poison dart frog); keney, cover background, interior background; Anto03, cover (poison dart frog icon); bennytrapp, pp. 3, 4; Marius, p. 6; janstria, p. 7; Andreas, p. 8; oscar garces, p. 9; Anneke, p. 10; F1 online digitale Bildagentur GmbH/ Alamy, pp. 10-11; kikkerdirk, pp. 11, 17 (poison dart frog), 23; phototrip.cz, p. 12; davemhuntphoto, p. 13; FotoCorn, p. 14; sebasdmarin/ iNaturalist, p. 15; Klaus Ulrich Müller/ Alamy, pp. 16-17; piemags/ nature/ Alamy, p. 17 (beetles); Patricio Murphy/ Wirestock, p. 17 (ants); Justin Philbois/ iNaturalist, p. 17 (fire-bellied snakes); Luan Faitanin Volpato/ Wikipedia, p. 17 (flies); Thorsten Spoerlein, pp. 18, 18-19; ondreicka, p. 20; Dan Olsen, p. 21.